Albert Einstein
Brilliant Scientist

written by Amanda Doering Tourville illustrated by Reed Sprunger

Content Consultant:
Freeman Dyson, Professor Emeritus,
Mathematical Physics and Astrophysics, Institute for Advanced Study

magic
Wagon

visit us at www.abdopublishing.com

Published by Magic Wagon, a division of the ABDO Group, PO Box 398166, Minneapolis, MN 55439.
Copyright © 2013 by Abdo Consulting Group, Inc. International copyrights reserved in all countries. All rights reserved. No part of this book may be reproduced in any form without written permission from the publisher.

Looking Glass Library™ is a trademark and logo of Magic Wagon.

Printed in the United States of America, North Mankato, Minnesota.
092012
012013

Text by Amanda Doering Tourville
Illustrations by Reed Sprunger
Edited by Holly Saari
Design and production by Emily Love

Library of Congress Cataloging-in-Publication Data

Tourville, Amanda Doering, 1980- author.
  Albert Einstein : brilliant scientist / written by Amanda Doering Tourville ; illustrated by Reed Sprunger.
    pages cm. – (Beginner biographies)
  Includes bibliographical references and index.
  ISBN 978-1-61641-937-0
1. Einstein, Albert, 1879-1955–Juvenile literature. 2. Physicists–Biography–Juvenile literature. I. Sprunger, Reed, illustrator. II. Title.
  QC16.E5T68 2013
  530.092–dc23
  [B]
                                                              2012023799

Table of Contents

Albert marveled at how the needle pointed north no matter which way he turned the compass.

4

Young Albert

Albert Einstein was born on March 14, 1879, in Ulm, Germany. He was the first child of Hermann and Pauline Einstein. In 1880, Albert's family moved to Munich, Germany.

Albert was a quiet child who didn't have many friends. He preferred to daydream or play with puzzles. Albert also enjoyed building with blocks and making houses out of playing cards.

When Albert was five, his father gave him a compass. As an adult, Albert would say that the compass taught him an important lesson. It made him realize that things can work in hidden ways.

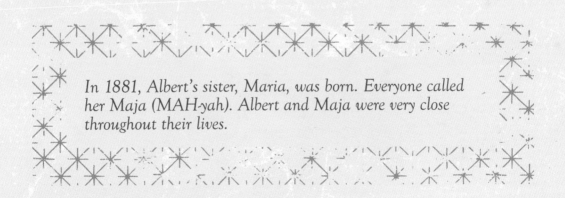

In 1881, Albert's sister, Maria, was born. Everyone called her Maja (MAH-yah). Albert and Maja were very close throughout their lives.

Albert used music to help him think.

Although the Einsteins were Jewish, Albert's parents sent him to a Catholic school. Albert earned good grades. But he didn't like how strict his teachers were. He didn't like having to memorize things or do classroom drills.

Instead, Albert liked to learn by asking questions. He began studying on his own. At age 12, he taught himself geometry, a type of math. In 1896, Albert finished high school. By this time, the Einsteins had moved to Aarau, Switzerland.

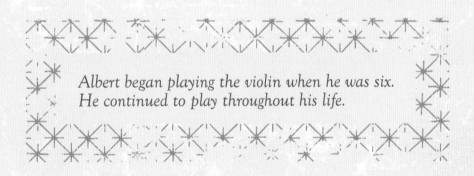

Albert began playing the violin when he was six. He continued to play throughout his life.

Curiosity

Albert Einstein was very interested in light. He once dreamed that he was traveling beside a beam of light. Einstein wondered what exactly light is. How does it travel? How fast can it go? Can anything travel faster than light?

At age 17, Einstein started college at the Swiss Federal Polytechnic School in Switzerland. He studied to become a math and science teacher. Einstein liked physics. This branch of science studies matter, energy, and light. Einstein often skipped classes to study physics on his own.

In a dream, Einstein traveled through space chasing a beam of light.

Einstein worked as a substitute teacher for two years.

Marriage and Money

At college, Einstein met Mileva Marić, who later became his wife. Einstein earned his teaching degree. But he had trouble finding a job. He wanted to work as an assistant to a professor at his college. Unfortunately, Einstein had argued with many of his professors or skipped too many of their classes. None of them offered him a job. Instead, Einstein taught as a substitute teacher and tutored students to earn a living.

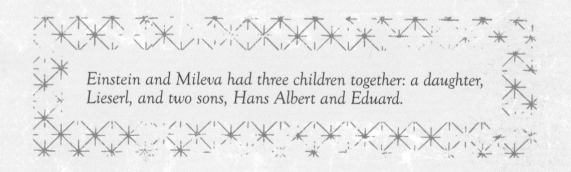

Einstein and Mileva had three children together: a daughter, Lieserl, and two sons, Hans Albert and Eduard.

Einstein worked on patents and his own science ideas at the Swiss Patent Office.

The Patent Office

In 1902, Einstein found a job at the Swiss Patent Office in Bern, Switzerland. He reviewed people's inventions to see if they should receive patents. Patents would protect them from having their ideas stolen.

Einstein enjoyed this position and was able to do his work quickly. He had spare time to think about physics. Einstein began figuring out the answers to his questions about light.

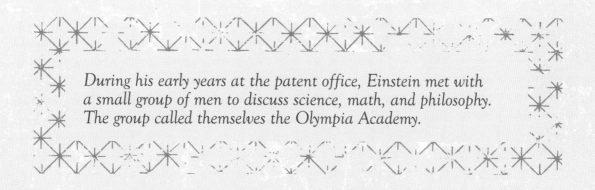

During his early years at the patent office, Einstein met with a small group of men to discuss science, math, and philosophy. The group called themselves the Olympia Academy.

Einstein believed light traveled as particles, not as waves, as most scientists thought.

The Miracle Year

The year 1905 is often called Einstein's "miracle year." He earned a doctorate in physics from the University of Zurich. Most important, he revealed his new ideas about light. These ideas would change the study of physics forever.

Before Einstein, scientists had thought light was like a wave. They believed it traveled the way ocean waves do. But Einstein said light was made up of tiny particles. They didn't flow together like a wave. Instead, the particles moved independently of each other. His idea was so hard to understand, it took 20 years for others to accept it.

Big Ideas about Light and Space

Einstein also said that light was the fastest thing in the universe. Nothing else, not even a spaceship, came close. In one second, light can travel around the equator almost eight times.

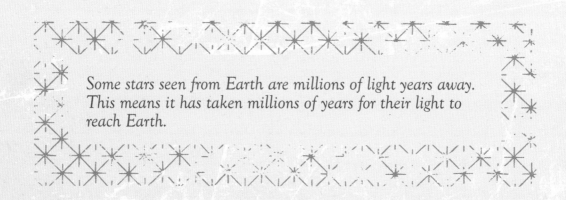

Some stars seen from Earth are millions of light years away. This means it has taken millions of years for their light to reach Earth.

Einstein was captivated by the mysteries of the universe.

Many scientists did not understand Einstein's ideas. But eventually they saw that Einstein was right. The science world began to pay attention to Einstein.

Einstein continued working as a professor. He took a teaching job at the German University in Prague in what is now the Czech Republic. In Prague, Einstein and Mileva often spent time with well-known artists and writers.

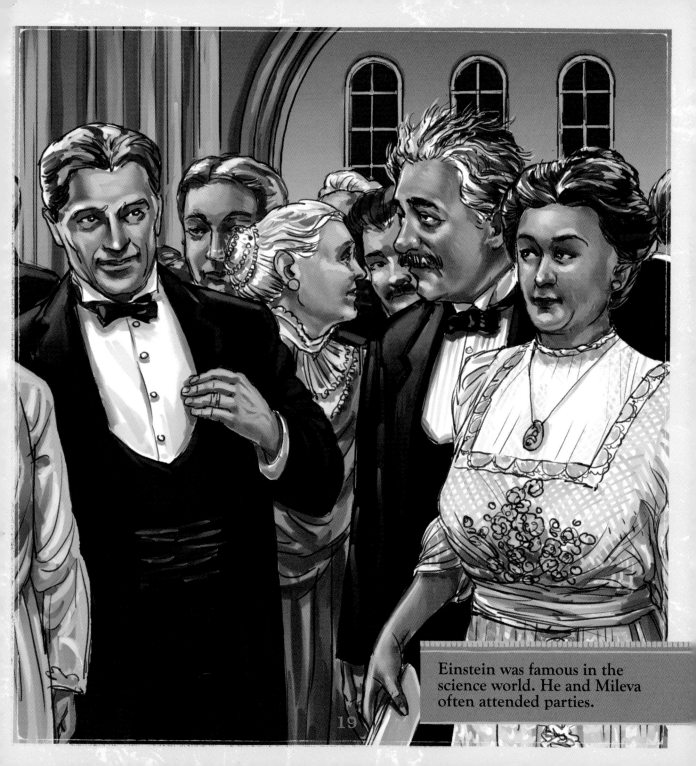

Einstein was famous in the science world. He and Mileva often attended parties.

The Eclipse

In 1915, Einstein had another big idea. He said that gravity could bend light. Some scientists did not believe Einstein. But the idea could be tested during a solar eclipse.

The world had to wait until 1919 for the eclipse. During the event, a scientist did experiments to test Einstein's idea about gravity bending light. Einstein was right again!

Einstein became famous around the world. When he traveled in Europe and the United States, thousands of people came to see him.

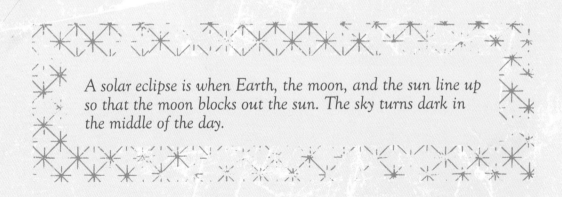

A solar eclipse is when Earth, the moon, and the sun line up so that the moon blocks out the sun. The sky turns dark in the middle of the day.

The solar eclipse in 1919 showed Einstein's idea was right.

Remarriage and Politics

Einstein had become a famous scientist, but his marriage was falling apart. In 1919, he and Mileva divorced. He then married his cousin, Elsa. He adopted Elsa's daughters, Ilse and Margot.

Einstein continued his work in physics. In 1921, he was awarded the Nobel Prize in physics. People recognized that his ideas about light particles were genius.

Einstein married Elsa in 1919.

World Affairs

In the 1920s and 1930s, Einstein spoke out against weapons, the military, and war. At that time, many people did not like Jews. Because Einstein was Jewish, some people treated him unfairly. Einstein spoke out against this discrimination.

Einstein came to believe that Jews should live in their own country. He supported those working to create a Jewish state in the Middle East. This nation would eventually be known as Israel.

Einstein spoke to audiences about science and public affairs.

In 1933, Adolf Hitler became the ruler of Germany. He wanted to create a master race of people that did not include Jews. During World War II, Hitler forced Jews into concentration camps.

Jews in Europe were not safe. Einstein and Elsa fled to the United States. Einstein became a U.S. citizen in 1940.

In 1945, World War II ended. But the war had changed some of Einstein's beliefs about peace. He realized that Germany needed to be stopped. He was no longer against all war.

Einstein and Elsa were safe in the United States during World War II.

A Legacy

In 1948, Israel became a country. In 1952, Einstein was asked to be president of the new Jewish state. Einstein was honored, but he turned it down.

Einstein died on April 18, 1955, in Princeton, New Jersey. Throughout his life, he worked to uncover some of the mysteries of the universe. He became world famous. Einstein is still remembered as one of the greatest scientists who ever lived.

Einstein spent time in his study trying to figure out answers to more of his science questions.

FUN FACTS

✦ Albert did not start talking until he was around three years old. Most children start talking shortly after one year.

✦ Einstein failed a physics class in college. This was partly because he did not show up for class.

✦ Only three people attended Einstein's first lecture in 1908. All three of these people were Einstein's coworkers.

✦ After his death, Einstein's brain was removed from his head in order to be studied.

✦ In 2000, *Time* magazine named Einstein the Person of the Century.

TIMELINE

1879 Albert Einstein was born on March 14 in Ulm, Germany.

1885 Albert began school and started taking violin lessons.

1896 Einstein finished high school in Aarau, Switzerland.

1900 Einstein graduated from the Swiss Federal Polytechnic School in Switzerland.

1902 Einstein was hired at the Swiss Patent Office.

1903 Einstein married Mileva Marić.

1905 Einstein published three important papers that changed physics forever.

1905 Einstein received his doctorate from the University of Zurich.

1909 Einstein became a professor at the University of Zurich.

1919 Scientists tested Einstein's theory during a solar eclipse. It was proven to be true.

1919 Einstein and Mileva divorced. He then married Elsa Einstein.

1921 Einstein was awarded the Nobel Prize in physics.

1940 Einstein became a U.S. citizen.

1955 Einstein died in Princeton, New Jersey, on April 18.

GLOSSARY

concentration camps—places people are forced to go without legal reasons.

discrimination—unfair treatment based on factors such as a person's race, religion, or gender.

doctorate—the highest educational degree someone can receive.

gravity—the force that pulls a smaller object toward a larger object.

Nobel Prize—an award for someone who has made outstanding achievements in his or her field of study.

particle—a very small piece of something.

physics—the science of studying matter, energy, and light.

tutor—someone who teaches a student privately.

World War II—from 1939 to 1945, fought in Europe, Asia, and Africa. Great Britain, France, the United States, the Soviet Union, and their allies were on one side. Germany, Italy, Japan, and their allies were on the other side.

LEARN MORE

At the Library

Lakin, Patricia. *Albert Einstein: Genius of the Twentieth Century*. New York: Aladdin, 2005.

Mattern, Joanne, and Laurence Santrey. *Albert Einstein, Creative Genius*. New York: Scholastic, 2005.

Venzia, Mike. *Albert Einstein: Universal Genius*. New York: Children's Press, 2009.

On the Web

To learn more about Albert Einstein, visit ABDO Group online at **www.abdopublishing.com**. Web sites about Einstein are featured on our Book Links page. These links are routinely monitored and updated to provide the most current information available.

INDEX